Saralynn Mercius

The Secret in the Attic

Copyright © 2025 Tega Joy Publishing LLC All rights reserved.

The Secret in the Attic.

First Edition. April 24th, 2025.

This is a work of fiction. Similarities to real people, animals, places, or events are entirely coincidental.

No part of this publication may be reproduced, stored in a retrieval system, or transmitted in any form or by any means, electronic, mechanical, photocopying, recording, or otherwise, without written permission of the copyright holder.

For information regarding permission, contact Tega Joy Publishing LLC.

TJP@TegaJoy.com

Chapter 1

Samantha arrived home after school to find her mom in her office, sipping tea while typing on her computer. She dropped her book bag on the floor and headed to the pantry to grab some cookies for a snack. Next, she retrieved a brown glass, restaurant-style cup from the cabinet and poured herself some chocolate milk from the fridge. Sitting down at the dining room table, she enjoyed her cookies and drink. Once she finished her snack, Samantha went to her room, changed her clothes, and lay down on her bed. She picked up the remote from her nightstand and turned on the TV.

A few moments later, Samantha heard a knock at the door. When it opened, she saw her mom, Tifi, standing there.

"Hey, why didn't you say hi?" Samantha's mom asked.

"I saw you were busy, so I thought it best to give you some space," Samantha mumbled.

"Oh, I see. Well, Samantha, I was wondering if you need all these toys and dolls," Tifi said, glancing around the room.

"No, not really, since I don't play with them anymore," Samantha replied.

"Alright, then it sounds like it's time to redecorate your room. You're going to middle school soon, and you'll need some new clothes, and maybe even a new phone," Tifi suggested.

"Yeah, that's true. Let's get these toys out of here first," Samantha said as she got off her bed.

"Sure, we can store them in the attic until we decide to donate them or something," Tifi agreed.

"Great! I'll head to the attic to grab some bags for my old clothes and toys," Samantha said as she walked out of her room.

"No, dear, that's alright. I'll get the bags. You focus on packing the clothes and toys," Tifi responded.

"Umm, okay," Samantha said.

Samantha's mom went to the attic and retrieved four large black bags. She returned to Samantha's room and began opening the wardrobe closet. As Tifi sorted through Samantha's toys and clothes, she placed them into the bags. Once they were filled, Samantha carried the bags to the attic while watching her mom.

"Mom," Samantha asked in a curious tone.

"Yes, honey?" Tifi replied.

"Why don't you let me go into the attic?" Samantha inquired.

"What makes you think I don't want you to go in the attic?" Tifi responded.

Samantha paused for a moment, contemplating how to answer thoughtfully. "Well, every time I bring up going into the attic, you say something that suggests I can't."

"True, but it's not that I don't want you up there," Tifi explained.

"Are you sure about that?" Samantha asked, raising her eyebrows and crossing her arms.

"Yes, it's just that attics can be a bit scary, you know," Tifi said.

"No, I don't know how scary an attic can be," Samantha replied.

"I mean, it's dark and cold, with spiderwebs," Tifi remarked.

"Then why don't you clean it?" Samantha shrugged.

"There's no point in cleaning it; it's an attic, and it will just get dirty again," Tifi replied.

"So what? We live in a house, and you clean it no matter how much it gets dirty. Take the dishes, for example," Samantha countered.

"The difference is that you can go into the attic whenever you want," Tifi said with a sigh.

"Can I go in there now?" Samantha inquired.

"No, I haven't cleaned the attic yet," Tifi responded, her voice shaky as she broke into a sweat.

"Are you hiding something?" Samantha asked, locking eyes with her mother.

"No, why would I?" Tifi said, glancing at her watch. "Come on, let's eat dinner. I heard you have a test tomorrow."

"Because you're acting strange," Samantha pointed out.

"Fine, I'll tell you the truth. I don't like going into the attic myself, and I am not comfortable with you going in there," Tifi responded hesitantly as she shifted awkwardly from one side to the other.

"Okay, fine. Can my friend come over tomorrow after school?" Samantha asked, hoping her mother would agree.

"Sure, just make sure you and your friend don't get into trouble or break anything while I'm not here," Tifi said as she began to set the dinner plates.

"Umm, okay," Samantha said.

Chapter 2

The next day, Samantha arrived home from school, bringing her friend Tanner along with her. As they entered the house, she remembered her mom wasn't there, so the house was hers to take care of. For a moment, she considered the possibility of using her allowance; she and Tanner could go somewhere fun, lowering the chance of breaking anything inside the house. Samantha went to the pantry to get snacks for Tanner and herself. Samantha got cupcake bites and some orange juice for herself, and she got Tanner some cookies with apple juice.

After Samantha and Tanner ate their snacks and drank their juice, they went to the living room to watch a little TV and talk. Samantha told Tanner about the attic. Piquing his interest, Tanner suggested they go to the attic right then.

Samantha wasn't sure. Her mom told her not to get into any trouble, and she knew her mom was hiding something. How would her mom feel when she learns they had gone into the attic? Heartbroken or hurt? Angered or upset? Either way, that was causing trouble, so she figured it was best not to go into the attic. Samantha just told Tanner that, no, they could not go into the attic, and they kept watching TV.

As evening approached, Tanner had to leave, leaving Samantha alone to eat dinner and watch TV. Samantha couldn't focus on what was going on with the show she was watching. She was too busy thinking about what could be in the attic and what her mom was hiding. Something was up there – but what? With all these thoughts swirling in her mind, she eventually fell asleep…waking to a scream on the TV because, somehow, the TV switched to a scary movie.

Samantha shrugged and went to get ready for bed. While she was walking to her room, she saw the attic door on the ceiling. Pausing for a moment, she thought of how badly she wanted to go up there...but then she decided against it.

It felt like it was calling her name. What was she to do? The voice wouldn't leave her alone, so she decided to call Tanner. He could surely help her solve this mystery!

A few minutes later, Tanner rang the doorbell. Samantha jumped. The doorbell startled her because it was so loud. She looked through the peephole and saw Tanner standing on the other side. Samantha opened the door and welcomed Tanner back in.

Samantha told Tanner she couldn't get the attic off her mind, especially with her mom acting suspiciously. So, she decided to go into the attic! Well, kind of. The voices in her head wouldn't leave her alone, or maybe it was God telling her she needed to know something.

Samantha cautiously pulled down the attic ladder and climbed up, with Tanner right behind. When she reached the landing at the top, she grabbed the door handle to open the attic...but it was locked! Samantha had never seen the attic door locked before! Now she knew for sure her mom was hiding something. Why else would it be necessary for her to lock the attic door? As Tanner reached the top of the ladder, Samantha showed him the lock on the door.

Samantha knew that the only way forward was to look for a key. It was getting late, and Samantha's mom would be coming home soon, so Samantha told Tanner he had to leave. Besides, she knew that her mom would not be too thrilled to see Tanner still visiting at such a late hour.

Tanner helped Samantha put the ladder back up into the ceiling, and then he left. Samantha cleaned the dishes and tidied the kitchen, so her mother would think she had done something useful and not suspect anything bad, like trying to go into the attic. Then she brushed her teeth, washed her face, took a bath, and went to bed.

Chapter 3

The next morning, Samantha woke up to find her mom still asleep. Wanting to keep her distance for a little longer, she decided to make some cereal for breakfast before heading to school. Usually, her mom would prepare a balanced meal, believing that cereal was only for those too lazy to cook something healthier. However, Samantha was doing her best to stay out of her mom's way, fearing that she might discover her secret attempt to get into the attic the night before.

She went to the cabinet to grab a bowl and spoon, then opened the fridge to pour some milk before heading to the pantry for her favorite cereal: Fruit Loops. Samantha loved the taste of Fruit Loops, though she wasn't entirely sure what made them so delicious—perhaps it was the mix of fruity flavors. She poured the colorful cereal into the bowl and added the vanilla milk.

She ate quickly, determined to catch the bus on time and avoid her mom's questions about the attic. Samantha realized she needed to come up with an excuse for her actions. If her mom ever found out that she had tried (unsuccessfully) to get into the attic, she wouldn't have a valid reason for her actions. That would surely lead to trouble! Just as she was lost in thought, her mom appeared in the kitchen, dressed in her blue robe, yawning as she made her way over to where Samantha was eating.

"Hi honey, what are you doing?" Tifi asked.

"Eating my cereal," Samantha said, shaky, and her tone was nervous.

"Are you okay?" Tifi asked.

"Yeah, but I have to go catch the bus and go to school," Samantha said, standing up from the table and grabbing her bowl and spoon to put them in the sink.

"OK, make sure you put the milk back in the fridge and cereal back in the pantry. Sometimes you put them both in the fridge," Tifi said, yawning as she walked back to her room.

"Oh yeah, sorry about that, Mom," Samantha said, putting her milk and cereal up.

Once she put away her cereal and milk, Samantha went to the bus stop.

After school that day, Samantha quietly entered the house. She tiptoed to her room, quietly closed the door, and lay on her bed, letting her mind wander about what her mother was hiding from her. Samantha sighed. Maybe she was unnecessarily working herself up. She needed to have fun and take her mind off this mystery. She checked her watch and realized it was 5 p.m. She had to go say hi to her mom before her mom got worried. Samantha left her room and looked for her mom, but she didn't see her anywhere in the house. She was probably at work again. Samantha decided to call Tanner over once more.

An hour later, the doorbell rang. Samantha opened the door and saw Tanner.

"What took so long?" Samantha asked, opening the door.

Tanner shrugged. "What did you call me for? Are we going to find a way to go into the attic again?"

"Hello?! No, I am trying to forget about why the attic bothers me. If I go up there, then I might get in trouble."

"Ok, then why am I here?" Tanner said, welcoming himself into the house and sitting down on the couch.

"Because I'm so bored, I thought you would have something fun to do." Samantha sat down with Tanner.

"Well, I got nothing fun for us to do besides explore the attic," Tanner said.

"What? I already said no," Samantha insisted.

"Your mother will never find out, so what's the harm in a little fun?" Tanner asked.

"I would get in trouble. Besides, if my Mom is already acting suspiciously, do you really think the attic will be fun? There could be anything up there!" Samantha said.

After an hour of sitting with nothing to do, Samantha and Tanner decided to watch a show called *Sister Sister*, which was Samantha's favorite. Tanner hated it. He didn't watch it. Instead, he just scrolled on his phone.

After Samantha watched 2 episodes of her show, Tanner said, "I'm so bored. Why can't we explore the attic?"

"I'm telling you for the last time, I don't want my Mom to find out I'm going into the attic," Samantha said in an impatient tone.

"Ok, but she didn't find out about anything we did the other day, so why don't we go in the attic? Don't you want to find out what she's hiding?" Tanner said in a pleading voice.

"No, just because she may not find out now doesn't mean she won't ever find out. What hides in the dark always comes to the light", Samantha said in a smart voice.

"Same for your mom, Samantha. Whatever hides in the dark comes out into the light. You need to find out what she's hiding." Tanner crossed his arms.

After a little while of Tanner pleading with Samantha to go into the attic, Samantha gave in, but she knew she had to be prepared for two things:
    1. What was in the attic.

2. Her mom finding out that she had discovered what was hiding in the attic.

Samantha led Tanner to her mom's office because she thought it was a good place for her mom to hide the attic key. She first searched through her mom's file drawers. Only files - nothing suspicious, and no attic key. Boring. Who would want to go through all those papers? Samantha thought to herself.

Could something important be hidden inside them? Samantha and Tanner decided to look through the files. While examining the last file, Tanner made a strange face.

"What's wrong?" Samantha asked.

"What's a key doing in a stack of papers?" Tanner asked.

"I dunno. Maybe it leads to the attic," Samantha suggested.

"Then what are we waiting for?! Let's get on up there!" Tanner exclaimed gleefully, dashing off towards the attic.

Samantha sighed and said, "I hope there isn't anything scary up there." Little did she know that once she entered the attic, her life would never be the same again. Whether for better or worse is to be debated…

Samantha and Tanner pulled down the ladder and climbed up to the attic door. Tanner used the key to unlock the door.

"Why do you get the honor of unlocking the door? It's my attic," Samantha pointed out.

"Well, you're too scared of this attic to come up here anyway," said Tanner.

"I am NOT scared," Samantha remarked in an impatient tone.

"So now that the door is unlocked, open it!" Tanner said, irritated.

Samantha pushed past Tanner and opened the door. They both stepped inside and looked around. It was a tiny attic, smaller than Samantha's bedroom, with a skylight at the top. It was very, very clean, contrary to what Samantha's mom had said. No cobwebs, no dust, no mice, nothing at all. A very clean floor, sparkling clean walls, and it was not even dark. In the corner sat the black bags filled with Samantha's old toys from the other day when Tifi had helped Samantha clean her room. Besides that, there sat a little treasure chest in the middle of the floor. That was all there was in the attic.

"All your concern about this?" Tanner asked, opening one of the black bags and pulling out a baby doll. "I thought you were too old for this little doll," he said, trying to hold back his laughter.

"Not funny," Samantha said, feeling a bit disappointed that the attic really held no secrets at all. So, what was her mother trying to hide? There was nothing up here! And it wasn't even spooky or dirty like her mom had led her to believe. Why on earth lock the attic if there was nothing in it to hide?

"So, what do you think your mom is hiding here?" Tanner asked. "It looks like a normal attic…well, I guess not completely normal because it's too clean! My attic has cobwebs and dust, and it's really cluttered and dark."

"How am I supposed to know?" Samantha asked. Meanwhile, Tanner had opened the treasure chest and began pulling out a purse, a scarf, and a flip phone that was probably 15 years old. He also pulled out a stack of files and papers, which he examined with a funny expression on his face.

"What's up now," Samantha asked.

"Oh, it's nothing. I just wonder why your name is on this file, " Tanner said, as he read it.

"Let me see," Samantha said, snatching the paper.

"I was reading that." Tanner crossed his arms in protest.

"Well, now I'm reading it," Samantha said, looking into the file.

Samantha examined the yellow file labeled 'Samantha.' Inside, it read:

> Dear Tifi,
>
> It's time to reveal the truth to Samantha, and I believe you know what I'm referring to. It's better to show her before it becomes too late. Please heed my advice; otherwise, she may be heartbroken forever

and might not trust you until she gets much older.

From,
Child Services

Samantha read the file, but she felt confused. Just behind the first letter was another document that stated:

Dear Tifi,

I told you to tell Samantha the truth, or it would shatter her. Her mom has passed away, so I suggest you tell her about this before she finds out, at the very least. Be honest and share the truth with her.

From,
Child Services

Samantha was so confused! What was going on? The questions started to come like an avalanche!

"Am I adopted? How is my mom dead? Who is my mom? Who is this lady taking care of me now? Why would she hide something like this?" Unable to speak, Samantha handed Tanner the letters in silence, her face frozen in shock. After Tanner read them, he stared at Samantha in silence.

"Are you ok?" Tanner asked, worried.

Samantha nodded, but both she and Tanner knew it was a lie. Samantha stared at the floor, remaining silent. "Let's just get out of here," Samantha said, tears streaming down her face.

"Wait, no, we can't stop. We found something interesting here; there might be more for us to discover," Tanner said.

"I said, 'Let's go; we're done looking.' I should have listened to Mom about this," Samantha said, crying.

"Fine, I'm going home. It's my dinner time", Tanner said, a bit upset.

"Bye," Samantha said, still crying a bit.

Chapter 4

Samantha tried to go to bed that night, but she couldn't sleep. She couldn't stop thinking about what had happened that day.

She had so many questions and wanted to tell her mom what she had done. However, she knew her mom would respond with, "I told you not to go in the attic, but you didn't listen, so now you've got your questions bothering you," and so on, blah, blah, blah…

Samantha had no clue what to do. Her dad had passed away years ago, and she didn't want to talk to Tanner. But then, when Samantha thought of her dad, she asked herself: Was he even my dad? Samantha felt so confused and betrayed. Who is this woman who claims to be my mother? How are there pictures of me all over this house when I was born if she's not really my mom? How can this be a lie? Is this whole life a lie? Samantha wondered. Am I A LIE OR A DREAM?

Samantha began to cry, feeling confused because she had no idea what was going on.

Samantha thought it might be best to tell her mom since she couldn't handle this anymore, and perhaps her mom would explain what it was about. But was it worth the risk to ask her mom? Samantha wondered. She walked into the kitchen and saw her mom opening the refrigerator door.

"Hey dear, how are you? Are you hungry?" Tifi said, peeking from the fridge. "Oh, honey, have you been crying? What's wrong?" Tifi walked up to Samantha, lifting her head.

Samantha stared at her mom, confused, struggling to find the right words to say but not finding them. Tifi looked into her daughter's eyes. Her eyes were filled with confusion, and in need of guidance and support.

"Speak your mind, Samantha," Tifi said with a reassuring smile.

Samantha saw her smile, and a tear rolled down her cheek. "Is Mom dead?"

Tifi let go of Samantha's face and stared at her, confused. Silence filled the room.

"What do you mean, dear?" Tifi's eyes were full of fear.

Samantha cried very hard. "Stop lying. I know the truth. Admit it, so-called mom." Samantha stomped her foot in anger.

"Please, dear, calm down. I'm sorry," Tifi said with tear-filled eyes. "I should have told you, but I was scared. Your mom died, and I thought you wouldn't find out. I thought it was best not to bring up such a thing that only brings tears and pain. And since you were too young to remember her, I thought it was for the best. I'm sorry," Tifi said, her eyes full of tears as they streamed down her face.

Samantha cried, "How could you? How could you lie to me for 14 years?!" She pushed Tifi away, tears of betrayal streaming down her face. Running down the hallway, she opened the door to her room, dashed inside, and slammed it shut. Samantha kicked her desk hard and cried out in pain.

After about an hour of crying, Samantha fell asleep, heartbroken. When her alarm clock rang at six o'clock, she picked it up and threw it against the wall. Rolling over, she refused to get out of bed. By the time Tifi came into Samantha's room, it was already after nine o'clock. Tifi opened the door, crossed the room to her bed, and gently nudged her, trying to rouse her from bed.

"Samantha, get up. You're late for school." Tifi shook her.

"Who cares about school when I discover the biggest secret of my life, and you can't even tell me the truth?" Samantha slowly sat up. Her face was as pale as snow, and her eyes were tired and dark. She looked around and lay back down in bed.

"Honey, do you want to stay home today and get some rest?" Tifi asked.

Samantha ignored her and rolled over. She got out of bed when she heard her mom leave the room and went to the bathroom. Looking in the mirror, Samantha saw that she looked like a mess, but she didn't care; she was still upset, angry, and betrayed. She sighed and lay back in bed. Grabbing her phone, she scrolled through TikTok. She noticed a lot of people posting pictures of themselves and their moms doing fun things. That's when it hit her that it was Mother's Day, and she started to cry. She didn't have a mother to celebrate Mother's Day with.

Samantha cried and cried. Then she heard the hot dog truck pulling up next to the neighbor's sidewalk to sell hot dogs in the neighborhood. Samantha went to the window and looked outside. The light was so bright that it felt like it would blind her. She closed the curtains and lay back down on her bed, feeling confused, tired, and upset.

Tifi knocked on the door, but Samantha said nothing.

Tifi opened the door and tried to make small talk with Samantha. "Hey, Samantha, want some food? Do you want a hot dog or something else?"

Samantha rolled over again, completely ignoring the question. She asked, "Why did you adopt me? Are you part of my family, like an aunt or grandma or something?"

Tifi sighed and said, "Why don't we talk while we eat?"

"No, I'm not hungry," Samantha said.

"But you haven't eaten all day, and it's lunch time," Tifi said.

"I'm not hungry," Samantha said. "Answer the question."

Tifi sighed and said, "Well, I'm your aunt, and your mother was my sister. When you were born, I was there because your dad was a pig and wasn't there for you. I supported your mom, but after you were born, she was never quite the same. She was always tired and didn't have energy, so I was always around to help take care of you. One day, your mom wouldn't eat or do anything; she just lay in bed. I sent her to the hospital, but they didn't know what was wrong with her. She stayed in the hospital for a long time. When you were three, she died. They were going to send you to a foster home, but I wanted you to have a normal childhood, so I adopted you. I told you that your mother was your aunt and that you were my daughter. You always remembered me as your mother because I have always been with you, even when you were young."

Samantha stared in disbelief at what had happened. How could she forget such an important memory? It was all coming back to her slowly. She couldn't believe she had forgotten this memory. She had seen her mom before and was beginning to remember her face.

Samantha was on the verge of tears, but she told Tifi to leave because she needed time to think. She felt deeply betrayed by her mother, yet perhaps she could find it in herself to forgive her. Her story seemed like it was something she needed to do for Samantha's benefit, but was it worth lying for all those years?

Tifi left, leaving Samantha alone to think. Yet all that Samantha could do was cry.

Chapter 5

Over the next couple of days, all Samantha could do was cry and lie in bed, staring around her dark room. She stopped going to school and stopped looking at her phone. Every day, she woke up paler and weaker than the day before. Tifi brought food to her room every day until one day, Samantha stopped eating altogether. Tifi knew she needed to shake things up and that it was her job to cheer Samantha up.

Samantha was lying in bed asleep when Tifi knocked on the door. Tifi burst in because Samantha was usually not asleep at this time, so she thought Samantha was just ignoring her. When Tifi woke Samantha up, Samantha slowly sat up. "What?" Samantha said in a weak voice.

"It's time you got out of this house and go somewhere fun so get ready," Tifi said cheerfully.

"No," Samantha said, laying back down.

"Look, I know you're upset about your mom and about how you couldn't celebrate Mother's Day, but today, why don't we make it Daughter's Day? That way, your mother from heaven can see you happy with her aunt. That would be the perfect Mother's Day gift for her. So what do you say, Samantha?" Tifi said, looking at Samantha's face as she sat on her bed. "I can wash your face, make it shine again, and we can put makeup on you, do your hair, and go somewhere fun."

Samantha said, "Fine, I´ll get my clothes, brush my teeth, and you can do the rest. Then we can leave this house."

"Good, that's what I want to hear, but first, eat," Tiff said, running out of the room and bringing a big, pretty, pink tray with breakfast.

Samantha took a good look at the food, drooling. She hadn't eaten for a long time and was quite starving, but she couldn't feel it because she was so sad. However, when she saw the food on the tray, oh boy, her hunger returned. The food looked amazing and smelled delicious too. It was an abundant stack of buttered pancakes with whipped cream and berries, bacon and eggs, and a clear, fancy glass of what looked like orange juice.

"Yeah, you know you want to eat this delicious-looking and smelling food, so eat it, dear, before it gets cold. And get ready; you need an appetite before we go have fun," Tifi said, handing the tray to Samantha.

"Thanks," Samantha said, already eating the food and gobbling it down like a little gremlin. After Samantha ate, she felt stuffed and full, but the food was great; she was smiling, and her face was a bit brighter.

"There, you look better now, get ready," Tifi said, handing Samantha some clothes. Tifi handed Samantha a white tank top and a small white mini skirt.

After Samantha got dressed, she walked down the hall into the living room. It was very bright because there were two windows letting light into the room. Tifi was sitting on a rocking chair reading a book. Tifi peeked up from her book to see Samantha trying to cover her face from the lights.

"You know you don't like the lights right now because you locked yourself in your room laying in bed in the dark the whole time," Tifi said, getting a brush to brush Samantha's long, straight hair.

"Whatever Mom, but I want to know where we are going to do whatever you think is fun."

Tifi smiled reassuringly, her eyes glimmering with joy. "Whatever you want, I just want you to be happy again and enjoy your life outdoors and not be locked in a room to live in and get depressed, so please, Samantha, let's go and do something nice."

"But first, I want to know where my mother's grave is, to see where she was buried. I want to see her face," Samantha said, thinking of her mother again and starting to get sad.

Samantha's sentence startled Tifi. "Why are you thinking of her grave right now?"

Samantha sighed, "Just please let me see her grave; I just want to see her and where she was buried."

"Ok fine," Tifi sighed.

Chapter 6

As Samantha visited her mother's grave, she felt an overwhelming wave of sadness. She stood there, staring at the name etched in stone, and couldn't believe this was how she had to reconnect—with silence and cold marble. She felt angry. Hurt. Deceived. She had known her mom once, but her aunt had kept the truth hidden for so long.

"This is messed up," Samantha whispered, biting her lip to hold back tears. She turned to Tifi and asked if they could go home.

At first, her aunt hesitated; however, seeing the pain in Samantha's eyes, she finally nodded.

When they got back, Samantha went straight to her room, hoping for peace. But the moment she opened the door, she froze.

There, gently sitting on her bed, was a glowing figure made of soft, golden light. It wasn't scary—it was calm and warm. Familiar. The figure raised a hand and waved.

Samantha blinked. The light shimmered, revealing her face more clearly now—kind, strong, beautiful.

"...Mom?" Samantha asked, voice trembling.

The angel smiled and nodded.

The figure got up, walked over to her desk, and picked up a pen. Then it wrote something on a piece of paper.

It said: **Hi.**

Samantha dropped the paper. "Wait... for real?"

The figure nodded slowly.

She didn't know whether to cry, hug it, or run out of the room; instead, she just stood there. "I thought you were gone."

The angel (because that's what it had to be—an angel) smiled at her, not with a mouth but in a glowing kind of way.

She turned around and yelled, "Aunt Tifi!! Come here!!"

Tifi came running in. "What? What is it?"

"Look! My mom is here. She's right there, sitting by the desk. She waved at me and wrote on the paper! Look!"

Tifi looked at the desk, then back at Samantha. "Samantha… there's nothing there."

"What? Yes, there is, she's right there!" Samantha pointed. "She waved. She wrote '*hi.*' Look at the paper!"

Tifi picked it up. "There's nothing on this, baby. It's blank."

"No it's not, it said—" Samantha snatched the paper back, but now it really *was* blank. Just white.

Tifi sighed and put a hand on Samantha's shoulder. "Sweetie, this is a lot...but I don't think there was anything to see."

"I saw her!" Samantha shouted, stepping back. "She was right there, and she waved at me!"

But when she turned around, the glowing figure was gone.

Samantha's heart sank. "No. No, come back," she whispered. "Please come back."

Tifi tried to hug her, but Samantha moved away.

"I don't want to talk," she mumbled.

Tifi seemed like she wanted to say more but didn't. She left the room quietly.

Samantha sat on her bed for a long time, her hands shaking. She didn't understand what had just happened; it felt real. It *was* real. Even if no one else believed her.

She lay down and hugged her pillow. She stared at the ceiling.

And even though her mom wasn't there anymore, the room still felt warm. Not like heater warm. But like... love.

Like something was still there.

She whispered, "Please don't leave me," and then fell asleep.

Chapter 7

The next day, Samantha didn't want to get out of bed. Not for school, not for food, not for anything. She just lay there thinking about her mom. About how she showed up for real, and how no one believed her. Not Tifi, not anyone.

At lunch, Tifi knocked. "You hungry?"

"No."

"You can't just lay in bed forever, Samantha."

"Watch me."

Tifi sighed. "Fine, but let me know when you're ready to talk...or just sit."

Samantha rolled over and faced the wall. "You don't get it."

There was quiet. Then the door closed.

Later that night, when the house was dark, Samantha sat at her desk. She pulled out the paper again. The one that had gone blank.

She whispered, "If you're still here… please come back."

Slowly, the words appeared, **Meet me in the attic.**

Samantha quietly slipped out of her bedroom, down the hall, and headed to the attic, making sure that Tifi did not hear her.

When she was in the attic, Samantha said softly, "Mom? I'm here!"

The air in the room got warm again. Not scary. Just soft.

Then the angel appeared again, smiling.

Samantha gasped. "Mom?"

The angel nodded.

Samantha ran over and hugged her. She felt it—like hugging sunshine.

"I missed you," she whispered.

The angel didn't talk with words. Just feelings. Warmth. Peace. Samantha felt them like messages in her heart.

Samantha stood there talking to the angel. She talked about school, Tifi, and her experiences… she didn't even realize she was crying.

And her mom listened, just staying there, glowing and quiet, yet full of love.

When at last her mom's angel faded away, Samantha looked around the room. The angel was gone. But the room still felt like her.

Days passed. Her mom came back a few more times to visit Samantha in the attic. Just short visits. Sometimes to hug her. Sometimes to listen. Sometimes to hear about Samantha's homework.

And Samantha started seeing things differently.

Like… maybe Tifi wasn't the enemy. Maybe she was just upset too and trying to do her best.

The last time Samantha saw her mom's angel, she asked, "Do you think it's time I just forgive Aunt Tifi? I feel tired of being sad all the time."

Her mother simply nodded, then faded away.

Chapter 8

The next morning, Samantha went downstairs and saw Tifi sitting at the table on her phone. She looked tired, like always.

"Hey," Samantha said.

Tifi looked up. "Morning."

There was a long pause.

Then Samantha asked, "You wanna go do something today? Just us?"

Tifi raised an eyebrow. "Like what?"

"I don't know. Mall? Ice cream? Something fun."

Tifi set her phone down. "You serious?"

"Yeah," Samantha said. "I think I'm done being mad."

Tifi smiled slightly. "Alright then. Let's go to the zoo."

They arrived before lunch, and the first thing they did was get ice cream cones, even though it was still kind of early. Tifi chose chocolate, while Samantha picked cotton candy flavor. It melted all over her fingers, but she didn't mind.

They walked through the monkey house, laughing as one of the monkeys waved at them. Next, they spotted the giraffes and stood there a while just watching them eat leaves.

They went to the petting zoo, too. Samantha fed a goat that tried to eat her sleeve.

Later, they got nachos from the snack stand and sat on a bench near the elephant area. The elephants were huge and kind of slow but looked peaceful. Samantha was having a lot of fun!

When they got back to the car, Samantha said, "This was actually kinda fun."

Tifi smiled. "Told you."

Samantha looked out the window. "I miss her."

"I know," Tifi said. "I do too."

"But I think she'd want us to be okay."

"She would," Tifi said.

Samantha nodded. Then she leaned over and gave Tifi a hug. For the first time in forever.

"I love you, Aunt Tifi," she said.

"I love you too, Samantha."

Then they drove home with the windows down and music on low. It was a good day.

And that was the start of something better.

Made in the USA
Columbia, SC
04 May 2025